PAUL
THEROUX

SLOW TRAINS TO SIMLA

PENGUIN BOOKS

PENGUIN BOOKS

Published by the Penguin Group. Penguin Books Ltd, 27 Wrights Lane, London
w8 5TZ, England. Penguin Books USA Inc., 375 Hudson Street, New York,
New York 10014, USA. Penguin Books Australia Ltd, Ringwood, Victoria, Australia.
Penguin Books Canada Ltd, 10 Alcorn Avenue, Toronto, Ontario, Canada M4V 3B2.
Penguin Books (NZ) Ltd, 182–190 Wairau Road, Auckland 10, New Zealand ·
Penguin Books Ltd, Registered Offices: Harmondsworth, Middlesex, England · These
extracts are from *The Great Railway Bazaar*, by Paul Theroux, published in Penguin
Books 1977. This edition published 1996. Copyright © Paul Theroux, 1975. All
rights reserved · Typeset by Rowland Phototypesetting Ltd, Bury St Edmunds,
Suffolk. Printed in England by Clays Ltd, St Ives plc ·
10 9 8 7 6 5 4 3 2 1

CONTENTS

The Khyber Mail to Lahore Junction

Rashid, the conductor on the sleeping car, helped me find my compartment, and after a moment's hesitation he asked me to have a look at his tooth. It was giving him aches, he said. The request was not impertinent. I had told him I was a dentist. I was getting tired of the Asiatic inquisition: Where do you come from? What do you do? Married or single? Any children? This nagging made me evasive, secretive, foolish, an inventor of cock-and-bull stories. Rashid made the bed and then opened up, tugging his lip down to show me a canine gnawed with decay.

'You'd better see a dentist in Karachi,' I said. 'In the meantime chew your food on the other side.'

Satisfied with my advice (and I also gave him two aspirins), he said, 'You will be very comfortable here. German carriage, about fifteen years old. Heavy, you see, so no shaking.'

It had not taken long to find my compartment. Only three were occupied – the other two by army officers – and my name was on the door, printed large on a label. Now I could tell on entering a train what sort of a journey it would be. The feeling I had on the Khyber Mail was slight disappointment that the trip would be so short – only twelve hours to Lahore. I wished it were longer: I had everything I needed. The compartment was large, well lighted, and comfortable, with a toilet and sink in an adjoining room; I had a drop-leaf table, well-upholstered seat, mirror, ashtray, chrome gin-bottle holder, the works. I was alone. But if I wished to have company I could stroll to the dining car or idle in the passage with the army officers. Nothing is expected of the train passenger. In planes the traveller is condemned to hours in a tight seat; ships require high spirits and sociability; cars and buses are unspeakable. The sleeping car is the most painless form of travel. In *Ordered South*, Robert Louis Stevenson writes,

Herein, I think, is the chief attraction of railway travel. The speed is so easy, and the train disturbs so little the scenes through which it takes us, that our heart becomes full of the placidity and stillness of the country; and while the body is being borne forward in the flying chain of carriages, the thoughts alight, as the humour moves them, at unfrequented stations . . .

The romance associated with the sleeping car derives from its extreme privacy, combining the best features of a cupboard with forward movement. Whatever drama is being enacted in this moving bedroom is heightened by the landscape passing the window: a swell of hills, the surprise of mountains, the loud metal bridge, or the melancholy sight of people standing under yellow lamps. And the notion of travel as a continuous vision, a grand tour's succession of memorable images across a curved earth – with none of the distorting emptiness of air or sea – is possible only on a train. A train is a vehicle that allows residence: dinner in the diner, nothing could be finer.

'What time does the Khyber Mail get to Karachi?'

'Timetable says seven-fifteen in the night,' said Rashid. 'But we will be five and a half hours late.'

'Why?' I asked.

'We are always five and a half hours late. It is the case.'

I slept well and was awakened at six the following

morning by a Sikh with a steel badge pinned to his turban that read *Pakistan Western Railways*. His right eye was milky with trachoma.

'You wanting breakfast?'

I said yes.

'I coming seven o'clock.'

He brought an omelette, tea, and toast, and for the next half-hour I sprawled, reading Chekhov's wonderful story 'Ariadne' and finishing my tea. Then I snapped up the shade and flooded the compartment with light. In brilliant sunshine we were passing rice fields and stagnant pools full of white lotuses and standing herons. Farther on, at a small tree, we startled a pair of pistachio-green parrots; they flew up, getting greener as they rose. Looking out a train window in Asia is like watching an unedited travelogue without the obnoxious soundtrack; I had to guess at the purpose of activities – people patting pie-shaped turds and slapping them on to the side of a mud hut to dry; men with bullocks and submerged ploughs, preparing a rice field for planting; and at Badami Bagh, just outside Lahore, a town of grass huts, cardboard shelters, pup tents, and hovels of paper, twigs, and cloth, everyone was in motion – sorting fruit, folding clothes, fanning the fire, shooing a dog away, mending a roof. It is the industry of the poor in the morning, so busy they look hopeful, but it is deceptive. The position of their settlement gives them away; this is the extreme of poverty, the shantytown by the railway tracks.

The shantytown had another witness: a tall thin Indian of about twenty, with long hair, stood at the corridor window. He asked me the time; his London accent was unmistakable. I asked him where he was headed.

'India. I was born in Bombay, but I left when I was three or four. Still, I'm an Indian right the way through.'

'But you were brought up in England.'

'Yeah. I've got a British passport too. I didn't want to get one, after all they did to me. But an Indian passport is too much trouble. See, I want to go to Germany eventually – they're in the Common Market. It's easy with a British passport.'

'Why not stay in London?'

'You can stay in London if you like. They're all racialists. It starts when you're about ten years old, and that's all you hear – wog, nigger, blackie. There's nothing you can do about it. At school it's   5 really terrible – ever hear about Paki-bashing? And I'm not even a Pakistani. They don't know the difference. But they're cowards. When I'm with me mate no one comes up and says nothing, but lots of times about ten blokes would start trouble with me. I hate them, I'm glad to be here.'

'This is Pakistan.'

'Same thing. Everyone's the same colour.'

'Not really,' I said.

'More or less,' he said. 'I can relax here – I'm free.'

'Won't you feel rather anonymous?'

'The first thing I'm going to do in India is get a haircut; then no one will know.'

It seemed a cruel fate. He spoke no Indian language, his parents were dead, and he was not quite sure how to get to Bombay, where he had some distant relatives who seldom replied to letters unless he enclosed money. He was one of those colonial anomalies, more English than he cared to admit, but uneasy in the only country he understood.

'In England they were always staring at me. I hated it.'

'I get stared at here,' I said.

'How do *you* like it?' I could see he was reproaching me with my colour; after all, he was almost home.

I said, 'I rather enjoy it.'

'Sahib.' It was Rashid, with my suitcase. 'We are approaching.'

'He calls you sahib,' said the Indian. He looked disgusted. 'He's afraid of you, that's why.'

'Sahib,' said Rashid. But he was speaking to the Indian. 'Now, please show me your ticket.'

The Indian was travelling second class. Rashid evicted him from first as the train drew in.

At Lahore Junction I stepped out (Rashid was at my side apologizing for the train's being late) into a city that was familiar: it matched a stereotype in my memory. My image of the Indian city derives from Kipling, and it was in Lahore that Kipling came of age as a writer. Exaggerating the mobs, the vicious bazaar, the colour and confusion, the Kipling of the early stories and *Kim* is really describing Lahore today, that side of it beyond the Mall where processions of rickshaws, pony carts, hawkers, and veiled women fill the narrow lanes and sweep you in their direction. The Anarkali Bazaar and the walled city, with its fort and mosques, have 7 retained the distracted exoticism Kipling mentions, though now, with a hundred years of repetition, it is touched with horror.

'Bad girls here,' said the *tonga* driver when he dropped me in a seedy district of the old city; but I saw none, and nothing resembling a Lahore house. The absence of women in Pakistan, all those cruising males, had an odd effect on me. I found myself staring, with other similarly idle men, at garish pictures of film stars, and I began to think that the strictures of Islam would quickly make me a fancier of the margins of anatomy, thrilling at especially trim ankles, seeking a wink behind a veil, or watching for a response in the shoulders of one of those shrouded forms. Islam's denials seemed capable of turning the most normal soul into a foot fetishist, and as if to combat this the movie posters lampooned the erotic: fat girls in boots struggling helplessly with hairy, leering men; tormented women clutching their breasts, Anglo-Indians (regarded as 'fast') swinging their bums and crooning into microphones. The men in Lahore stroll with their eyes upturned to these cartoon fantasies.

'They invite you out to eat,' an American told me. This was at the spectacular fort, and we were both admiring the small marble pavilion, called *Naulakha* (Kipling named his house outside Brattleboro, Vermont, after it, because it was so expensive to build: 'naulakha' means 900,000). The American was agitated. He said, 'You finish eating and they start eyeballing your chick. It's always your chick they're after. The chick's strung out. "Gee, Mohammed, why don't you have any pockets in your *dhoti*?" "We are not having any pockets, miss" – that kind of crap. One guy – this really pissed me off – he takes me aside and says, "*Five minutes! Five minutes!* That's all I want with her!" But would he let me have *his* chick for five minutes? You've gotta be joking.'

The order in Lahore is in the architecture, the moghul and colonial splendour. All around it are crowds of people and vehicles, and their dereliction makes the grandeur emphatic, as the cooking fat and cow-dung makes the smells of perfume and joss-sticks keener. To get to the Shalimar Gardens I had to pass through miles of congested streets of jostling people with the starved look of predators. I shouldered my way through the venereal township of Begampura; but inside the gardens it is peaceful, and though it has been stripped of its marble, and 9 the reflecting pools are dark brown, the gardens have the order and shade – a sense of delicious refuge – that could not be very different from that imagined by Shah Jahan, when he laid them out in 1637. The pleasures of Lahore are old, and though one sees attempts everywhere, the Pakistanis have not yet succeeded in turning this beautiful city into a ruin.

Ramadhan continued, and the restaurants were either closed or on emergency rations, eggs and tea. So I was forced into an unwilling fast too, hoping it wouldn't drive me crazy as it manifestly did the Afghan and Pakistani. Instead of somnolence, hunger produced excitable, glassy-eyed individuals, some of whom quick-marched from alleyways to clutch my sleeve.

'Pot – hashish – LSD.'

'LSD?' I said. 'You sell LSD?'

'Yes, why not? You come to my place. Also nice copper, silver, handicraft.'

'I don't want handicraft.'

'You want hashish? One kilo twenty dollar.'

It was tempting, but I preferred bottled mango juice, which was sweet and thick, and the curry puffs known as *samosas*. The *samosas* were always wrapped in pages from old school copybooks. I sat down, drank my juice, ate my *samosa*, and read the wrapper: '. . . the shearing force at any [grease mark] on the Beam is represented by the Vertical Distance between that Line and the Line CD.'

There were forty-seven tables in the dining room of Faletti's Hotel. I found them easy to count because I was the only diner present on the two evenings I ate there. The five waiters stood at various distances from me, and when I cleared my throat two would rush forward. Not wanting to disappoint them I asked them questions about Lahore, and in one of these conversations I learned that the Punjab Club was not far away. I thought it would be a good idea to have a postprandial snooker game, so on the second evening I was given directions by one of the waiters and set off for the club.

I lost my way almost immediately in a district adjacent to the hotel where there were no street lights. My footsteps roused the watchdogs and as I walked these barking hounds leaped at fences and hedges. I have not conquered a childhood fear of strange dogs, and, although the trees smelled sweet and the night was cool, I had no idea where I was going. It was ten minutes before a car approached. I flagged it down.

'You are coming from?'

'Faletti's Hotel.'

'I mean your country.'

'United States.'

'You are most welcome,' said the driver. 'My name is Anwar. May I give you a lift?'

'I'm trying to find the Punjab Club.'

'Get in please,' he said, and when I did, he said, 'How are you please?' This is precisely the way the posturing Ivan Turkin greets people in Chekhov's story 'Ionych'.

Mr Anwar drove for another mile, telling me how fortunate it was that we should meet – there were a lot of thieves around at night, he said – and at the Punjab Club he gave me his card and invited me to his daughter's wedding, which was one week away. I said I would be in India then.

'Well, India is another story altogether,' he said, and drove off.

The Punjab Club, a bungalow behind a high hedge, was lighted and looked cosy, but it was completely deserted. I had imagined a crowded bar, a lot of cheerful drinkers, a snooker game in progress, a pair in the corner plotting adultery, waiters with trays of drinks, and chits flying back and forth. This could have been a clinic of some kind; there was not a soul in sight, but it had the atmosphere – and even the magazines – of a dentist's waiting room. I saw what I wanted a few doors along a corridor: large red letters on the window read WAIT FOR THE STROKE, and in the shadows were two tables, the balls in position, ready for play under a gleaming rack of cues.

'Yes?' It was an elderly Pakistani, and he had the forlorn abstraction of a man interrupted in his reading. He wore a black bow tie, and the pocket of his shirt sagged with pens. 'What can I do for you?'

'I just happened to be passing,' I said. 'I thought I might stop in. Do you have reciprocal privileges with any clubs in London?'

'No, not that I know of.'

'Perhaps the manager would know.'

'I am the manager,' he said. 'We used to have an arrangement with a club in London – many years ago.'

'What was the name of it?'

'I'm sorry, I've forgotten, but I know the club is no longer in existence. What was it you wanted?' 13

'A game of snooker.'

'Who would you play with?' He smiled. 'There is no one here.'

He showed me around, but the lighted empty rooms depressed me. The place was abandoned, like Faletti's dining room with its forty-seven empty tables, like the district where there were only watch-dogs. I said I had to go, and at the front door he said, 'You might find a taxi over there, in the next road but one. Good night.'

It was hopeless. I had walked about a hundred yards from the club and could not find the road, though I was going in the direction he had indicated. I could hear a dog growling behind a near-by hedge. Then I heard a car. It moved swiftly towards me and screeched to a halt. The driver got out and opened the back door for me. He said the manager had sent him to take me back to my hotel; he was afraid I'd get lost.

I set off in search of a drink as soon as I got back to the hotel. It was still early, about ten o'clock, but I had not gone fifty yards when a thin man in striped pyjamas stepped from behind a tree. His eyes were prominent and lighted in the dusky triangle of his face.

'What are you looking for?'

'A drink.'

'I get you a nice girl. Two hundred rupees. Good fucking.' He said this with no more emotion than a man hawking razor blades.

'No thanks.'

'Very young. You come with me. Good fucking.'

'And good fucking to you,' I said. 'I'm looking for a drink.'

He tagged along behind me, mumbling his refrain, and then at an intersection, by a park, he said, 'Come with me – in here.'

'In there?'

'Yes, she is waiting.'

'In those trees?' It was black, unlighted and humming with crickets.

'It is a park.'

'You mean I'm supposed to do it there, under a tree?'

'It is a *good* park, sahib!'

A little farther on I was accosted again, this time by a young man who was smoking nervously. He caught my eye. 'Anything you want?'

'No.'

'A girl?'

'No.'

'Boy?'

'No, go away.'

He hesitated, but kept after me. At last he said softly, '*Take me.*'

A twenty-minute walk did not take me any closer to a bar. I turned, and, giving the pimps a wide berth, went back to the hotel. Under a tree in front three old men were hunched around a pressure lamp, playing cards. One saw me pass and called out, 'Wait, sahib!' He turned his cards face down and trotted over to me.

'No,' I said before he opened his mouth.

'She's very nice,' he said.

I kept walking.

'All right, only two hundred and fifty rupees.'

'I know where I can get one for two hundred.'

'But this is in your room! I will bring her. She will stay until morning.'

'Too much money. Sorry.'

'Sahib! There are expenses! Ten rupees for your sweeper, ten also for your *chowkidar*, ten for your bearer, *baksheesh* here and there. If not, they will make trouble. Take her! She will be very nice. My girls are experienced in every way.'

'Thin or fat?'

'As you like. I have one, neither thin nor fat, but like this.' He sketched a torso in the air with his fingers, suggesting plumpness. 'About twenty-two or twenty-three. Speaks very good English. You will like her so much. Sahib, she is a trained nurse!'

He was still calling out to me as I mounted the steps to the hotel's verandah. It turned out that the only bar in Lahore was the Polo Room in my hotel. I had an expensive beer and fell into conversation with a young Englishman. He had been in Lahore for two months. I asked him what he did for amusement. He said there wasn't very much to do, but he was planning to visit Peshawar. I told him Peshawar was quieter than Lahore. He said he was sorry to hear that because he found Lahore intolerable. He was bored, he said, but there was hope. 'I've got an application pending at the club,' he said. He was a tall plain fellow, who blew his nose at the end of every sentence. 'If they let me in, I think I'll be all right. I can go there in the evenings – it's a pretty lively place.'

'What club are you talking about?'

'The Punjab Club,' he said.

The Frontier Mail

Amritsar, two taxi rides from Lahore (the connecting train hasn't run since 1947), is on the Indian side of the frontier. It is to the Sikh what Benares is to the Hindu, a religious capital, a holy city. The object of the Sikh's pilgrimage is the Golden Temple, a copper-gilt gazebo in the centre of a tank. The tank's sanctity has not kept it from stagnation. You can smell it a mile away. It is the dearest wish of every Sikh to see this temple before he dies and to bring a souvenir back from Amritsar. One of the favourite souvenirs is a large multi-coloured poster of a headless man. Blood spurts from the stump of his neck; he wears the uniform of a warrior. In one hand he carries a sword, in the other he holds his dripping head. I asked nine Sikhs what this man's name was. None could tell me, but all knew his story. In one of the Punjab wars he was decapitated. But he was very determined. He picked up his head, and, holding it in his hand so that he could see what he was doing (the eyes of the severed head blaze with resolution), he continued to fight. He did this so that he could get back to Amritsar and have a proper cremation. This story exemplifies the Sikh virtues of piety, ferocity, and strength. But Sikhs are also very kind and friendly, and an enormous number are members of Lions Club International. This is partly a cultural misunderstanding, since all Sikhs bear the surname Singh, which means lion; they feel obliged to join.

Special underpants are required by the Sikh religion, along with uncut hair, a silver bangle, a wooden comb, and an iron dagger. And as shoes are prohibited at the Golden Temple, I hopped down the hot marble causeway, doing a kind of firewalker's tango, watching these leonine figures stripped to their holy drawers bathing themselves in the tank and gulping the green water, swallowing grace and dysentery in the same mouthful. The Sikhs are great soldiers and throughout the temple enclosure there are marble tablets stating the fact that the Poona Horse Regiment and the Bengal Sappers contributed so many thousand rupees. For the rest of the Indians, Gujaratis in particular, Sikhs are yokels, and jokes are told to illustrate the simplicity of the Sikh mind. There is the one about the Sikh who, on emigrating to Canada, is told that he must prove himself a true Canadian by going into the forest and wrestling a bear and raping a squaw. He sets out and returns a month later, with his turban in tatters and his face covered with scratches, saying, 'Now I must wrestle the squaw.' Another concerns a Sikh who misses his bus. He chases the bus, trying to board, and soon realizes he has run all the way home. 'I've just chased my bus and saved fifty paisas,' he tells his wife, who replies, 'If you had chased a taxi you could have saved a rupee.'

I had a meal at a Sikh restaurant after wandering around the city and then went to the railway station to buy my ticket on the Frontier Mail to Delhi. The man at Reservations put me on the waiting list and told me there was 'a 98 per cent chance' that I would get a berth, but that I would have to wait until half-past four for a confirmation. Indian railway stations are wonderful places for killing time in, and they are like scale models of Indian society, with its divisions of caste, class, and sex: SECOND-CLASS LADIES' WAITING ROOM, BEARERS' ENTRANCE, THIRD-CLASS EXIT, FIRST-CLASS

TOILET, VEGETARIAN RESTAURANT, NON-

VEGETARIAN RESTAURANT, RETIRING ROOMS, CLOAKROOM and the whole range of occupations on office signboards, from the tiny one saying SWEEPER, to the neatest of all, STATION-MASTER.

A steam locomotive was belching smoke at one of the platforms. I crossed over and as I snapped a picture a Sikh appeared on the footplate and asked me to send him a print. I said I would. He asked me where I was going, and when I told him I was taking the Frontier Mail he said, 'You have so many hours to wait. Come with me. Get in this bogie' – he pointed to the first car – 'and at the first station you can come in here and ride with me.'

'I'm afraid I'll miss my train.'

'You will not,' he said. 'Without fail.' He said this precisely, as if remembering an English lesson.

'I don't have a ticket.'

'No one is having a ticket. They are all cheating!'

So I climbed aboard and at the first station joined him in the cab. The train was going to Atari, on the Pakistan border, sixteen miles away. I had always wanted to ride in the engine of a steam locomotive, but this trip was badly timed. We left just at sunset and as I was wearing my prescription sunglasses – 21 my other pair was in my suitcase in the station cloakroom – I could not see a thing. I held on, blind as a bat, sweating in the heat from the firebox. The Sikh shouted explanations of what he was doing, pulling levers, bringing up the pressure, spinning knobs, and dodging the coal shoveller. The noise and the heat prevented me from taking any pleasure in this two-hour jaunt, and I suppose I must have looked dispirited because the Sikh was anxious to amuse me by blowing the whistle. Every time he did it the train seemed to slow down.

My face and arms were flecked with soot from the ride to Atari. On the Frontier Mail this was no problem, and I had the enjoyable experience that humid evening of taking a cold shower, squatting on my heels under the burbling pipe, as the train tore through the Punjab to Delhi.

I returned to my compartment to find a young man sitting on my berth. He greeted me in an accent I could not quite place, partly because he lisped and also because his appearance was somewhat bizarre. His hair, parted in the middle, reached below his shoulders; his thin arms were sheathed in tight sleeves and he wore three rings with large orange stones on each hand, bracelets of various kinds and a necklace of white shells. His face frightened me: it was that corpselike face of lunacy or a fatal illness, with sunken eyes and cheeks, deeply lined, bloodless, narrow, and white. He had a cowering stare, and as he watched me – I was still dripping from my shower – he played with a small leather purse. He said his name was Hermann; he was going to Delhi. He had bribed the conductor so that he could travel with a European. He didn't want to be in a compartment with an Indian – there might be trouble. He hoped I understood.

'Of course,' I said. 'But do you feel all right?'

'I have been sick – four days in Amritsar I have been in the hospital, and in Quetta also. I was so nervous. The doctors take tests and they give me this medicine, but it does no good. I don't sleep, I don't eat – just maybe glass of milk and piece of bread. I fly to Amritsar from Lahore. I was so sick in Lahore – three days in hospital and in Quetta two days. I cross Baluchistan. Yazd, you know Yazd? It is a terrible place. Two nights I am there and I am on the bus two days from Teheran. I cannot sleep. Every five hours the bus stops and I take some tea and a little melon. I am sick. The people say, "Why 23 you don't talk – are you angry?" But I say, "No, not angry, but sick –"'

This was the way he spoke, in long lisped passages, interrupting himself, repeating that he was sick in a voice that was monotonously apologetic. He was German and had been a sailor, a deck hand on a German ship, then a steward on a Finnish one. He had sailed for seven years and had been to the States – 'Yes, to every country,' he said, 'but only for a few hours.' He loved ships, but he couldn't sail any more. I asked why. 'Hepatitis,' he said, giving it a German pronunciation. He caught it in Indonesia and was in the hospital for weeks. He had never managed to shake it off: he still needed tests. He'd had one in Amritsar. 'People say to me, "Your face is sick." I know my face is sick, but I cannot eat.'

His face was ghastly, and he was trembling. 'Are you taking any medicine?'

'No.' He shook his head. 'I take this.' He opened the leather purse he had been smoothing with his scrawny fingers and took out a cellophane envelope. He peeled the cellophane away and showed me a wad of brown sticky stuff, like a flattened plug of English toffee.

'What is it?'

'Opium,' he said. 'I take it in little balls.'

His lisp made 'balls' moistly vicious.

'I am a yunk.' He broke off a piece of opium and rolled it between his fingers, slowly making it a pellet.

'A junkie?'

'Yes, I take needle. See my arms.'

He locked the compartment door and pulled the curtain across the window. He rolled up his left sleeve. His arm appalled me: each vein was clearly defined by dark bruised scars of needle marks, thick welts that made the veins into black cords. He touched his arm shyly, as if it didn't belong to him and said, 'I cannot get heroin. In Lahore I am not feeling so well. I stay in hospital but still I am weak and nervous. The people are making noise and it is so hot. I don't know what I can do. So I escape and I walk down the street. A Pakistani says to me he has some morphine. I go with him and he shows me. It is good – German morphine. He asks me for one hundred and fifty rupees. I give him and take an injection. That is how I get to Amritsar. But in Amritsar I get very sick and I cannot get any more of morphine. So I take this –' He patted his right pocket and took out a cake of hashish, roughly the size of the opium blob, but dry and cracked. 'Or I smoke this –' He withdrew a little sack of marijuana.

I told him that with his budget of drugs he was lucky to have got into India. At the border post I had seen an Indian customs official ask a boy to drop his jeans.

'Yes,' said Hermann. 'I am so nervous! The man asks me do I have pot and I say no. Do I smoke it? I say, yes, sometimes, but he doesn't look at my luggages. If I am nervous I can hide it in secret places.'

'Then I suppose you don't have anything to worry about.'

'No, I am hot and nervous always.'

'But you can hide your drugs.'

'I can even throw them away and buy more,' he said. 'But my arms! If they see my arms they know. I have to hide my arms always.' He pushed his sleeves up and looked again at the long dark scars.

He told me how it was that he had come to India. In Hanover, he decided to cure himself of his heroin habit. He registered as an addict and entered a rehabilitation centre – he called it 'The Release' – where he was given 700 Deutsche marks a month and a daily glass of methadone. In return for this he helped clean the centre. He never went out; he was afraid that if he did he would meet someone who'd sell him heroin. But an odd thing happened: by staying in he rarely spent his monthly allowance, and he found that at the end of a year he had saved quite a lot of money – enough to live on in India for six months or more. So he packed up and left, just like that, on a charter flight to Teheran, where his withdrawal symptoms began.

He had carried his dereliction to a derelict land. He was doomed, he stank of death, and his condition was not so different from that of the unfortunates who appeared at the railway stations we passed, gathering for the light and water. There are foreigners who, knowing they are wrecked, go to India to be anonymous in her decrepitude, to age and sicken in the *bustees* of the East. They are people, V. S. Naipaul wrote recently, 'who wish themselves on societies more fragile than their own . . . who in the end do no more than celebrate their own security'.

'I take this now.' He popped the pellet of opium into his mouth and closed his eyes. 'Then I take some water.' He drank a glass of water. He had already drunk two, and I realized that the Indian water would kill him if the drugs didn't. 'Now I sleep. If I don't sleep I take another opium.'

Twice during the night a match flared in the upper berth, lighting the fan on the ceiling. I heard the crackle of cellophane, the snap of the gummy opium in his fingers, and Hermann gulping water.

The signs in Amritsar Station (THIRD-CLASS EXIT, SECOND-CLASS LADIES' WAITING ROOM, FIRST-CLASS TOILET, SWEEPERS ONLY) had given me a formal idea of Indian society. The less formal reality I saw at seven in the morning in the Northern Railways Terminal in Old Delhi. To understand the real India, the Indians say, you must go to the villages. But that is not strictly true, because the Indians have carried their villages to the railway stations. In the daytime it is not apparent – you might mistake any of these people for beggars, ticketless travellers (sign: TICKETLESS TRAVEL IS A SOCIAL EVIL), or unlicensed hawkers. At night and in the early morning the station village is complete, a community so preoccupied that the thou-
28 sands of passengers arriving and departing leave it

undisturbed: they detour around it. The railway dwellers possess the station, but only the new arrival notices this. He feels something is wrong because he has not learned the Indian habit of ignoring the obvious, making a detour to preserve his calm. The newcomer cannot believe he has been plunged into such intimacy so soon. In another country this would all be hidden from him, and not even a trip to a village would reveal with this clarity the pattern of life. The village in rural India tells the visitor very little except that he is required to keep his distance and limit his experience of the place to tea or a meal in a stuffy parlour. The life of the village, its interior, is denied to him.

But the station village is all interior, and the shock of this exposure made me hurry away. I didn't feel I had any right to watch people bathing under a low faucet – naked among the incoming tide of office workers; men sleeping late on their *charpoys* or tucking up their turbans; women with nose rings and cracked yellow feet cooking stews of begged vegetables over smoky fires, suckling infants, folding bedrolls; children pissing on their toes; little girls, in oversized frocks falling from their shoulders, fetching water in tin cans from the third-class toilet;

and, near a newspaper vendor, a man lying on his back, holding a baby up to admire and tickling it. Hard work, poor pleasures, and the scrimmage of appetite. This village has no walls. I distracted myself with the signs, GWALIOR SUITINGS, RASHMI SUPERB COATINGS, and the film poster of plump faces that was never out of view, BOBBY ('A Story of Modern Love'). I was moving so quickly I lost Hermann. He had drugged himself for the arrival: crowds made him nervous. He floated down the platform and then sank from view.

I wondered whether I would find any of this Indian candour familiar enough to ignore. I was told that I should not draw any conclusions from Delhi: Delhi wasn't India – not the real India. Well, I said, I had no intention of staying in Delhi. I wanted to go to Simla, Nagpur, Ceylon – to wherever there was a train.

'There is no train to Ceylon.'

'There's one on the map.' I unrolled my map and traced the black line from Madras to Colombo.

'*Acha*,' said the man. He wore a colourful hand-loomed shirt and he waggled his head from side to side, the Indian gesture – like a man trying to shake water out of his ears – that means he is listening with approval. But the man, of course, was an American. Americans in India practise these affectations to endear themselves to Indians, who seem so embarrassed by these easily parodied mannerisms that (at the American embassy at least) the liaison men say, 'We're locking you into that programme,' while the American looking on says, '*Acha*,' and giggles mirthlessly.

I was being locked into a programme: lectures in Jaipur, Bombay, Calcutta, Colombo. Wherever, I said, there was a train.

'There is no train to Colombo.'

'We'll see,' I said, and then listened to one of those strange conversations I later found so common as to be the mainstay of American small talk in India: The American on His Bowels. After the usual greetings and pauses these people would report on the vagaries of their digestive tracts. Their passion was graceless and they were as hard to silence as whoopee cushions.

'I had a bad night,' one embassy man said. 'The German ambassador gave a party. Delicious meal – it always is. All kinds of wine, umpteen courses, the works. But, God, I was up at five this morning, sick as a dog. Tummy upset.'

'It's a funny thing,' said another man. 'You have a good meal at some dirty little place and you know you're going to pay for it. I just came back from Madras. I was fine – and I had some pretty risky meals. Then I go to some diplomatic thing and I'm doubled up for days. So there's no telling where you'll get it.'

'Tell Paul about Harris.'

'Harris! Listen,' said the man, 'there was a fella here. Harris. Press Section. Went to the doctor. Guess why? He was constipated. *Constipated!* In *India!* It got around the embassy. People used to see him and laugh like hell.'

'I've been fine lately,' said a junior officer, holding his end up, as it were. 'Knock on wood. I've had some severe – I mean, really bad times. But I figured it out. What I usually do is have yogurt. I drink tons of the stuff. I figure the bacteria in yogurt keeps down the bacteria in lousy food. Kind of an equalizing thing.'

There was another man. He looked pale, but he said he was bearing up. Kind of a bowel thing. Up all night. Cramps. Delhi belly. Food goes right through you. He said, 'I had it in spades. Bacillary. Ever have bacillary? No? It knocked me flat. For

32

six days I couldn't do a thing. Running back and forth, practically living in the john.'

Each time the subject came up, I wanted to take the speaker by his hand-loomed shirt, and, shaking him, say, 'Now listen to me! There is absolutely nothing wrong with your bowels!'

The Kalka Mail for Simla

In spite of my dishevelled appearance, it was
thought by some in Delhi to be beneath my dignity
to stand in line for my ticket north to Simla, though
perhaps this was a tactful way of suggesting that
if I did stand in line I might be mistaken for an
Untouchable and set alight (these Harijan combus-
tions are reported daily in Indian newspapers). The
American official who claimed his stomach was col-
lapsing with dysentery introduced me to Mr Nath,
who said, 'Don't sweat. We'll take care of everything.' I had heard that one before. Mr Nath rang
his deputy, Mr Sheth, who told his secretary to ring
a travel agent. At four o'clock there was no sign of
the ticket. I saw Mr Sheth. He offered me tea. I
refused his tea and went to the travel agent. This
was Mr Sud. He had delegated the ticket-buying
to one of his clerks. The clerk was summoned. He
didn't have the ticket; he had sent a messenger, a
low-caste Tamil whose role in life, it seemed, was
to lengthen lines at ticket windows. An Indian story:

and still no ticket. Mr Nath and Mr Sud accompanied me to the ticket office, and there we stood ('Are you sure you don't want a nice cup of tea?') watching this damned messenger, ten feet from the window, holding my application. Bustling Indians began cutting in front of him.

'Now you see,' said Mr Nath, 'with your own eyes why things are so backwards over here. But don't worry. There are always seats for VIPs.' He explained that compartments for VIPs and senior government officials were reserved on every train until two hours before departure time, in case someone of importance might wish to travel at the last minute. Apparently a waiting list was drawn up every day for each of India's 10,000 trains.

'Mr Nath,' I said, 'I'm not a VIP.'

'Don't be silly,' he said. He puffed his pipe and moved his eyes from the messenger to me. I think he saw my point because his next words were, 'Also we could try money.'

'*Baksheesh*,' I said. Mr Nath made a face.

Mr Sud said, 'Why don't you fly?'

'Planes make me throw up.'

'I think we've waited long enough,' said Mr Nath.   35

'We'll see the man in charge and explain the situation. Let me do the talking.'

We walked around the barrier to where the ticket manager sat, squinting irritably at a ledger. He did not look up. He said, 'Yes, what is it?' Mr Nath pointed his pipe stem at me and, with the pomposity Indians assume when they speak to each other in English, introduced me as a distinguished American writer who was getting a bad impression of Indian Railways.

'Wait a minute,' I said.

'It is imperative that we do our utmost to ensure –'

'Tourist?' said the ticket manager.

I said yes.

He snapped his fingers. 'Passport.'

I handed it over. He wrote a new application and dismissed us. The application went back to the messenger, who had wormed his way to the window.

'It's a priority matter,' said Mr Nath crossly. 'You are a tourist. You have come all this way, so you have priority. We want to give favourable impression. If I want to travel with my family – wife, small children, maybe my mother too – they say, "Oh, no, there is a *tourist* here. Priority matter!"' He grinned without pleasure. 'That is the situation. But you have your ticket – that's the important thing, isn't it?'

The elderly Indian in the compartment was sitting cross-legged on his berth reading a copy of *Filmfare*. Seeing me enter, he took off his glasses, smiled, then returned to his magazine. I went to a large wooden cupboard and smacked it with my hand, trying to open it. I wanted to hang up my jacket. I got my fingers into the louvred front and tugged. The Indian took off his glasses again, and this time he closed the magazine.

'Please,' he said, 'you will break the air conditioner.'

'This is an air conditioner?' It was a tall box the height of the room, four feet wide, varnished, silent, and warm.

He nodded. 'It has been modernized. This carriage is fifty years old.'

'Nineteen twenty?'

'About that,' he said. 'The cooling system was very interesting then. Every compartment had its own unit. That is a unit. It worked very well.'

'I didn't realize there were air conditioners in the twenties,' I said.

'They used ice,' he said. He explained that blocks of ice were slipped into lockers under the floor – it was done from the outside so that the passengers' sleep would not be disturbed. Fans in the cupboard I had tried to open blew air over the ice and into the compartment. Every three hours or so the ice was renewed. (I imagined an Englishman snoring in his berth while at the platform of some outlying station Indians with bright eyes pushed cakes of ice into the lockers.) But the system had been converted: a refrigerating device had been installed under the blowers. Just as he finished speaking there was a whirr from behind the louvres and a loud and prolonged *whoosh*!

'When did they stop using ice?'

'About four years ago,' he said. He yawned. 'You will excuse me if I go to bed?'

The train started up, and the wood panelling of this old sleeping car groaned and creaked; the floor shuddered, the metal marauder-proof windows clattered in their frames, and the *whooshing* from the tall cupboard went on all night. The Kalka Mail 38 was full of Bengalis on their way to Simla for a festival, the Kali *puja*. Bengalis, whose complexion resembles that of the black goddess of destruction they worship, and who have the same sharp hook to their noses, have the misfortune to live at the opposite end of the country from the most favoured Kali temple. Kali is usually depicted wearing a necklace of human skulls, sticking her maroon tongue out, and trampling a human corpse. But the Bengalis were smiling sweetly all along the train, with their baskets of food and neatly woven garlands of flowers.

I was asleep when the train reached Kalka at dawn, but the elderly Indian obligingly woke me up. He was dressed and seated at the drop-leaf table, having a cup of tea and reading the *Chandigarh Tribune*. He poured his tea into the cup, blew on it, poured half a cup into the saucer, blew on it, and then, making a pedestal of his fingers, drank the tea from the saucer, lapping it like a cat.

'You will want to read this,' he said. 'Your vice president has resigned.'

He showed me the paper, and there was the glad news, sharing the front page with an item about a Mr Dikshit. It seemed a happy combination, Dikshit and Agnew, though I am sure Mr Dikshit's 39 political life had been blameless. As for Agnew's, the Indian laughed derisively when I translated the amount he had extorted into rupees. Even the black-market rate turned him into a cut-price punk. The Indian was in stitches.

In Kalka two landscapes meet. There is nothing gradual in the change from plains to mountains: the Himalayas stand at the upper edge of the Indo-Gangetic plain; the rise is sudden and dramatic. The trains must conform to the severity of the change; two are required – one large roomy one for the ride to Kalka, and a small tough beast for the ascent to Simla. Kalka itself is a well-organized station at the end of the broad-gauge line. Between the Himalayas and Kalka is the cool hill station of Simla on a bright balding ridge. I had my choice of trains for the sixty-mile journey on the narrow gauge: the toy train or the rail car. The blue wooden carriages of the train were already packed with pil-grims – the Bengalis, nimble at boarding trains, had performed the Calcutta trick of diving headfirst through the train windows and had got the best seats. It was an urban skill, this somersault – a fire drill in reverse – and it left the more patient hill people a bit glassy-eyed. I decided to take the rail car. This was a white squarish machine, with the face of a Model-T Ford and the body of an old bus. It was mounted low on the narrow-gauge tracks and had the look of a battered limousine. But considering that it was built in 1925 (so the driver assured me), it was in wonderful shape.

I found the conductor. He wore a stained white uniform and a brown peaked cap that did not fit him. He was sorry to hear I wanted to take the rail car. He ran his thumb down his clipboard to mystify me and said, 'I am expecting another party.'

There were only three people in the rail car. I felt he was angling for *baksheesh*. I said, 'How many people can you fit in?'

'Twelve,' he said.

'How many seats have been booked?'

He hid his clipboard and turned away. He said, 'I am very sorry.'

'You are very helpful.'

'I am expecting another party.'

'If they show up, you let me know,' I said. 'In the meantime, I'm putting my bag inside.'

'It might get stolen,' he said brightly.

'Nothing could please me more.'

41

'Wanting breakfast, sahib?' said a little man with a push-broom.

I said yes, and within five minutes my breakfast was laid out on an unused ticket counter in the middle of the platform, tea, toast, jam, a cube of butter, and an omelette. The morning sunlight struck through the platform, warming me as I stood eating my breakfast. It was an unusual station for India: it was not crowded, there were no sleepers, no encampment of naked squatters, no cows. It was filled that early hour with the smell of damp grass and wildflowers. I buttered a thick slice of toast and ate it, but I couldn't finish all the breakfast. I left two slices of toast, the jam, and half the omelette uneaten, and I walked over to the rail car. When I looked back, I saw two ragged children reaching up to the counter and stuffing the remainder of my breakfast into their mouths.

At seven-fifteen, the driver of the rail car inserted a long-handled crank into the engine and gave it a jerk. The engine shook and coughed and, still juddering and smoking, began to whine. Within minutes we were on the slope, looking down at the top of Kalka Station, where in the train yard two
42 men were winching a huge steam locomotive around

in a circle. The rail car's speed was a steady ten miles an hour, zigzagging in and out of the steeply pitched hill, reversing on switchbacks through the terraced gardens and the white flocks of butterflies. We passed through several tunnels before I noticed they were numbered; a large number 4 was painted over the entrance of the next one. The man seated beside me, who had told me he was a civil servant in Simla, said there were 103 tunnels altogether. I tried not to notice the numbers after that. Outside the car, there was a sheer drop, hundreds of feet down, for the railway, which was opened in 1904, is cut directly into the hillside, and the line above is notched like the skidway on a toboggan run, circling the hills.

After thirty minutes everyone in the rail car was asleep except the civil servant and me. At the little stations along the way, the postman in the rear seat awoke from his doze to throw a mailbag out the window to a waiting porter on the platform. I tried to take pictures, but the landscape eluded me: one vista shifted into another, lasting only seconds, a dizzying displacement of hill and air, of haze and all the morning shades of green. The meat-grinder cogs working against the rack under the rail car ticked like an ageing clock and made me drowsy. I took out my inflatable pillow, blew it up, put it under my head, and slept peacefully in the sunshine until I was awakened by the thud of the rail car's brakes and the banging of doors.

'Ten minutes,' said the driver.

We were just below a wooden structure, a doll's house, its window boxes overflowing with red blossoms, and moss trimming its wide eaves. This was Bangu Station. It had a wide complicated verandah on which a waiter stood with a menu under his arm. The rail-car passengers scrambled up the stairs. My Kalka breakfast had been premature; I smelled eggs and coffee and heard the Bengalis quarrelling with the waiters in English.

I walked down the gravel paths to admire the well-tended flower beds and the carefully mown lengths of turf beside the track; below the station a rushing stream gurgled, and signs there, and near the flower beds, read NO PLUCKING. A waiter chased me down to the stream and called out, 'We have juices! You like fresh mango juice? A little porridge? Coffee-tea?'

We resumed the ride, and the time passed quickly as I dozed again and woke to higher mountains, with fewer trees, stonier slopes, and huts perched more precariously. The haze had disappeared and the hillsides were bright, but the air was cool and a fresh breeze blew through the open windows of the rail car. In every tunnel the driver switched on orange lamps, and the racket of the clattering wheels increased and echoed. After Solon the only people in the rail car were a family of Bengali pilgrims (all of them sound asleep, snoring, their faces turned up), the civil servant, the postman, and me. The next stop was Solon Brewery, where the air was pungent with yeast and hops, and after that we passed through pine forests and cedar groves. On one stretch a baboon the size of a six-year-old crept off the tracks to let us go by. I remarked on the largeness of the creature.

The civil servant said, 'There was once a *saddhu* – a holy man – who lived near Simla. He could speak to monkeys. A certain Englishman had a garden, and all the time the monkeys were causing him trouble. Monkeys can be very destructive. The Englishman told this *saddhu* his problem. The *saddhu* said, "I will see what I can do." Then the *saddhu* went into the forest and assembled all the monkeys. He said, "I hear you are troubling the

45

Englishman. That is bad. You must stop; leave his garden alone. If I hear that you are causing damage I will treat you very harshly." And from that time onwards the monkeys never went into the Englishman's garden.'

'Do you believe that story?'

'Oh, yes. But the man is now dead – the *saddhu*. I don't know what happened to the Englishman. Perhaps he went away, like the rest of them.'

A little farther on, he said, 'What do you think of India?'

'It's a hard question,' I said. I wanted to tell him about the children I had seen that morning pathetically raiding the leftovers of my breakfast, and ask him if he thought there was any truth in Mark Twain's comment on Indians: 'It is a curious people. With them, all life seems to be sacred except human life.' But I added instead, 'I haven't been here very long.'

'I will tell you what I think,' he said. 'If all the people who are talking about honesty, fair play, socialism, and so forth – if they began to practise it themselves, India will do well. Otherwise there will be a revolution.'

He was an unsmiling man in his early fifties and had the stern features of a Brahmin. He neither drank nor smoked, and before he joined the civil service he had been a Sanskrit scholar in an Indian university. He got up at five every morning, had an apple, a glass of milk, and some almonds; he washed and said his prayers and after that took a long walk. Then he went to his office. To set an example for his junior officers he always walked to work, he furnished his office sparsely, and he did not require his bearer to wear a khaki uniform. He admitted that his example was unpersuasive. His junior officers had parking permits, sumptuous furnishings, and uniformed bearers.

'I ask them why all this money is spent for nothing. They tell me to make a good first impression is very important. I say to the blighters, "What about *second* impression?"'

'Blighters' was a word that occurred often in his speech. Lord Clive was a blighter and so were most of the other viceroys. Blighters ask for bribes; blighters try to cheat the Accounts Department; blighters are living in luxury and talking about socialism. It was a point of honour with this civil servant that he had never in his life given or received *baksheesh*: 'Not even a single paisa.' Some of his clerks had, and in eighteen years in the civil service he had personally fired thirty-two people. He thought it might be a record. I asked him what they had done wrong.

'Gross incompetence,' he said, 'pinching money, hanky-panky. But I never fire anyone without first having a good talk with his parents. There was a blighter in the Audit Department, always pinching girls' bottoms. Indian girls from good families! I warned him about this, but he couldn't stop. So I told him I wanted to see his parents. The blighter said his parents lived fifty miles away. I gave him money for their bus fare. They were poor, and they were quite worried about the blighter. I said to them, "Now I want you to understand that your son is in deep trouble. He is causing annoyance to the lady members of this department. Please talk to him and make him understand that if this continues I will have no choice but to sack him." Parents go away, blighter goes back to work, and ten days later he is at it again. I suspended him on the spot, then I charge-sheeted him.'

I wondered whether any of these people had tried to take revenge on him.

'Yes, there was one. He got himself drunk one night and came to my house with a knife. "Come outside and I will kill you!" That sort of thing. My wife was upset. But I was angry. I couldn't control myself. I dashed outside and fetched the blighter a blooming kick. He dropped his knife and began to cry. "Don't call the police," he said. "I have a wife and children." He was a complete coward, you see. I let him go and everyone criticized me – they said I should have brought charges. But I told them he'll never bother anyone again.

'And there was another time. I was working for Heavy Electricals, doing an audit for some cheaters in Bengal. Faulty construction, double entries, and estimates that were five times what they should have been. There was also immorality. One bloke – son of the contractor, very wealthy – kept four harlots. He gave them whisky and made them take their clothes off and run naked into a group of women and children doing *puja*. Disgraceful! Well, they didn't like me at all and the day I left there were four *dacoits* with knives waiting for me on the station road. But I expected that, so I took a different road, and the blighters never caught me. A month later two auditors were murdered by *dacoits*.'

The rail car tottered around a cliffside, and on the opposite slope, across a deep valley, was Simla.

Most of the town fits the ridge like a saddle made entirely of rusty roofs, but as we drew closer the fringes seemed to be sliding into the valley. Simla is unmistakable, for as *Murray's Handbook* indicates, 'its skyline is incongruously dominated by a Gothic Church, a baronial castle and a Victorian country mansion'. Above these brick piles is the sharply pointed peak of Jakhu (8,000 feet); below are the clinging house fronts. The southerly aspect of Simla is so steep that flights of cement stairs take the place of roads. From the rail car it looked an attractive place, a town of rusting splendour with snowy mountains in the background.

'My office is in that castle,' said the civil servant.

'Gorton Castle,' I said, referring to my handbook. 'Do you work for the Accountant General of the Punjab?'

'Well, I *am* the A.G.,' he said. But he was giving information, not boasting. At Simla Station the porter strapped my suitcase to his back (he was a Kashmiri, up for the season). The civil servant introduced himself as Vishnu Bhardwaj and invited me for tea that afternoon.

The Mall was filled with Indian vacationers taking their morning stroll, warmly dressed children, women with cardigans over their saris, and men in tweed suits, clasping the green Simla guidebook in one hand and a cane in the other. The promenading has strict hours, nine to twelve in the morning and four to eight in the evening, determined by mealtimes and shop openings. These hours were fixed a hundred years ago, when Simla was the summer capital of the Indian empire, and they have not varied. The architecture is similarly unchanged – it is all high Victorian, with the vulgarly grandiose touches colonial labour allowed, extravagant gutters and porticoes, buttressed by pillars and steelwork to prevent its slipping down the hill. The Gaiety Theatre (1887) is still the Gaiety Theatre (though when I was there it was the venue of a 'Spiritual Exhibition' I was not privileged to see); pettifogging continues in Gorton Castle, as praying does in Christ Church (1857), the Anglican cathedral; the viceroy's lodge (Rastrapati Nivas), a baronial mansion, is now the Indian Institute of Advanced Studies, but the visiting scholars creep about with the diffidence of caretakers maintaining the sepulchral stateliness of the place. Scattered among these large Simla buildings are the bungalows – Holly Lodge, Romney Castle, The Bricks, 51

Forest View, Sevenoaks, Fernside – but the inhabitants now are Indians, or rather that inherited breed of Indian that insists on the guidebook, the walking stick, the cravat, tea at four, and an evening stroll to Scandal Point. It is the Empire with a dark complexion, an imperial outpost that the mimicking vacationers have preserved from change, though not the place of highly coloured intrigues described in *Kim*, and certainly tamer than it was a century ago. After all, Lola Montez, the *grande horizontale*, began her whoring in Simla, and the only single women I saw were short red-cheeked Tibetan labourers in quilted coats, who walked along the Mall with heavy stones in slings on their backs.

I had tea with the Bhardwaj family. It was not the simple meal I had expected. There were eight or nine dishes: *pakora*, vegetables fried in batter, *poha*, a rice mixture with peas, coriander, and turmeric; *khira*, a creamy pudding of rice, milk, and sugar; a kind of fruit salad, with cucumber and lemon added to it, called *chaat*; *murak*, a Tamil savoury, like large nutty pretzels; *tikkiya*, potato cakes; *malai* chops, sweet sugary balls topped with cream; and almond-scented *pinnis*. I ate what I could, and the next day I saw Mr Bhardwaj's office in Gorton

Castle. It was as sparely furnished as he had said on the rail car, and over his desk was this sign:

> I am not interested in excuses for delay;
> I am interested only in a thing done.
>
> *Jawaharlal Nehru*

The day I left I found an ashram on one of Simla's slopes. I had been interested in visiting an ashram ever since the hippies on the Teheran Express had told me what marvellous places they were. But I was disappointed. The ashram was a ramshackle bungalow run by a talkative old man named Gupta, who claimed he had cured many people of advanced paralysis by running his hands over their legs. There were no hippies in this ashram, though Mr Gupta was anxious to recruit me. I said I had a train to catch. He said that if I was a believer in yoga I wouldn't worry about catching trains. I said that was why I wasn't a believer in yoga.

Mr Gupta said, 'I will tell you a story. A yogi was approached by a certain man who said he wanted to be a student. Yogi said he was very busy and had no time for man. Man said he was desperate. Yogi did not believe him. Man said he would commit

53

suicide by jumping from roof if yogi would not take him on. Yogi said nothing. Man jumped.

'"Bring his body to me," said yogi. Body was brought. Yogi passed his hands over body and after a few minutes man regained his life.

'"Now you are ready to be my student," said yogi. "I believe you can act on proper impulses and you have shown me great sincerity." So man who had been restored to the living became student.'

'Have you ever brought anyone to life?' I asked.

'Not as yet,' said Mr Gupta.

Not as yet! His guru was Paramahansa Yogananda, whose sleek saintly face was displayed all over the bungalow. In Ranchi, Paramahansa Y. had a vision. This was his vision: a gathering of millions of Americans who needed his advice. He described them in his *Autobiography* as 'a vast multitude, gazing at me intently' that 'swept actorlike across the stage of consciousness . . . the Lord is calling me to America . . . Yes! I am going forth to discover America, like Columbus. He thought he had found India; surely there is a karmic link between these two lands!' He could see the people so clearly, he recognized their faces when he arrived in California a few years later. He stayed in Los Angeles for thirty years, and, unlike Columbus, died rich, happy and fulfilled. Mr Gupta told me this hilarious story in a tone of great reverence, and then he took me on a tour of the bungalow, drawing my attention to the many portraits of Jesus (painted to look like a yogi) he had tacked to the walls.

'Where do you live?' asked a small friendly ash-ramite, who was eating an apple. (Simla apples are delicious, but, because of a trade agreement, the whole crop goes to Poland.)

'South London at the moment.'

'But it is so noisy and dirty there!'

I found this an astonishing observation from a man who said he was from Kathmandu; but I let it pass.

'I used to live in Kensington Palace Gardens,' he said. 'The rent was high, but my government paid. I was the Nepalese ambassador at the time.'

'Did you ever meet the queen?'

'Many times! The queen liked to talk about the plays that were on in London. She talked about the actors and the plot and so on. She would say, "Did you like *this* part of the play or that one?" If you hadn't seen the play it was very difficult to reply. 55

But usually she talked about horses, and I'm sorry to say I have no interest at all in horses.'

I left the ashram and paid a last visit to Mr Bhardwaj. He gave me various practical warnings about travelling and advised me to visit Madras, where I would see the real India. He was off to have the carburettor in his car checked and to finish up some accounts at his office. He hoped I had enjoyed Simla and said it was a shame I hadn't seen any snow. He was formal, almost severe in his farewell, but, walking down to Cart Road, he said, 'I will see you in England or America.'

'That would be nice. I hope we do meet again.'

'We will,' he said, with such certainty I challenged it.

'How do you know?'

'I am about to be transferred from Simla. Maybe going to England, maybe to the States. That is what my horoscope says.'

READ MORE IN PENGUIN

For complete information about books available from Penguin and how to order them, please write to us at the appropriate address below. Please note that for copyright reasons the selection of books varies from country to country.

IN THE UNITED KINGDOM: Please write to *Dept. EP, Penguin Books Ltd, Bath Road, Harmondsworth, Middlesex UB7 0DA.*

IN THE UNITED STATES: Please write to *Consumer Sales, Penguin USA, P.O. Box 999, Dept. 17109, Bergenfield, New Jersey 07621-0120.* VISA and MasterCard holders call 1-800-253-6476 to order Penguin titles.

IN CANADA: Please write to *Penguin Books Canada Ltd, 10 Alcorn Avenue, Suite 300, Toronto, Ontario M4V 3B2.*

IN AUSTRALIA: Please write to *Penguin Books Australia Ltd, P.O. Box 257, Ringwood, Victoria 3134.*

IN NEW ZEALAND: Please write to *Penguin Books (NZ) Ltd, Private Bag 102902, North Shore Mail Centre, Auckland 10.*

IN INDIA: Please write to *Penguin Books India Pvt Ltd, 706 Eros Apartments, 56 Nehru Place, New Delhi 110 019.*

IN THE NETHERLANDS: Please write to *Penguin Books Netherlands bv, Postbus 3507, NL-1001 AH Amsterdam.*

IN GERMANY: Please write to *Penguin Books Deutschland GmbH, Metzlerstrasse 26, 60594 Frankfurt am Main.*

IN SPAIN: Please write to *Penguin Books S. A., Bravo Murillo 19, 1° B, 28015 Madrid.*

IN ITALY: Please write to *Penguin Italia s.r.l., Via Felice Casati 20, I-20124 Milano.*

IN FRANCE: Please write to *Penguin France S. A., 17 rue Lejeune, F-31000 Toulouse.*

IN JAPAN: Please write to *Penguin Books Japan, Ishikiribashi Building, 2-5-4, Suido, Bunkyo-ku, Tokyo 112.*

IN GREECE: Please write to *Penguin Hellas Ltd, Dimocritou 3, GR-106 71 Athens.*

IN SOUTH AFRICA: Please write to *Longman Penguin Southern Africa (Pty) Ltd, Private Bag X08, Bertsham 2013.*